KETO CHAFFLE

RECIPES

COOKING BOOK 2021 WAFFLE,
HEALTHY AND APPETIZING, TO
LOSE WEIGHT WITH TASTE AND
MAINTAIN THE LIFESTYLE OF THE
KETOGEN DIET,TO LEARN TO COOK
THE HEALTHY WAY

TABLE OF CONTENTS

Additionally, the information in the following pages is intended only for informational purposes and should thus be thought of as universal. As befitting its nature, it is presented without assurance regarding its prolonged validity or interim quality. Trademarks that are mentioned are done without written consent and can in no way be considered an endorsement from the trademark holder.

BREAKFAST CHAFFLE RECIPES

Peanut Butter Cup Chaffles

Preparation Time: 5 minutes

Cooking Time: 15 minutes

Servings: 1

Ingredients:

For the chaffle:

- Eggs: 1
- Mozzarella cheese: ½ cup shredded
- Cocoa powder: 2 tbsp.
- Espresso powder: ¼ tsp.
- Sugar free chocolate chips: 1 tbsp.

For the filling:

- Peanut butter: 3 tbsp.
- Butter: 1 tbsp.
- Powdered sweetener: 2 tbsp.

Direction:

1. Add all the chaffle ingredients in a bowl and whisk

2. Preheat your mini waffle iron if needed and grease it
3. Cooking your mixture in the mini waffle iron for at least 4 minutes
4. Make two chaffles
5. Mix the filling ingredients together
6. When chaffles cool down, spread peanut butter on them to make a sandwich

Nutrition: Calories: 448; Total Fat: 34g; Carbs: 17g; Net Carbs: 10g; Fiber: 7g; Protein: 24g

Chocolaty Chaffles

Preparation Time: 5 minutes

Cooking Time: 15 minutes

Servings: 1

Ingredients:

- Eggs: 1
- Mozzarella cheese: ½ cup shredded
- Cocoa powder: 2 tbsp.
- Espresso powder: ¼ tsp.
- Sugar free chocolate chips: 1 tbsp.

Directions:

1. Add all the chaffle ingredients in a bowl and whisk
2. Preheat your mini waffle iron if needed and grease it
3. Cooking your mixture in the mini waffle iron for at least 4 minutes
4. Make as many chaffles as you can

Nutrition: Calories: 258; Total Fat: 23g; Carbs: 12g; Net Carbs: 6g; Fiber: 6g; Protein: 5g

Mc Griddle Chaffle

Preparation Time: 5 minutes

Cooking Time: 10 minutes

Servings: 2

Ingredients:

- Egg: 2
- Mozzarella cheese: 1½ cup (shredded)
- Maple Syrup: 2 tbsp. (sugar-free)
- Sausage patty: 2
- American cheese: 2 slices
- Swerve/Monkfruit: 2 tbsp.

Directions:

1. Preheat a mini waffle maker if needed and grease it
2. In a mixing bowl, beat eggs and add shredded Mozzarella cheese, Swerve/Monkfruit, and maple syrup
3. Mix them all well and pour the mixture to the lower plate of the waffle maker
4. Close the lid
5. Cooking for at least 4 minutes to get the desired crunch
6. Remove the chaffle from the heat

7. sausage patty by following the instruction given on the packaging
8. Place a cheese slice on the patty immediately when removing from heat
9. Take two chaffles and put sausage patty and cheese in between
10. Make as many chaffles as your mixture and waffle maker allow
11. Serve hot and enjoy!

Nutrition: Calories: 231; Total Fat: 20g; Carbs: 8g; Net Carbs: 6g; Fiber: 2g; Protein: 9g

Cinnamon Swirl Chaffles

Preparation Time: 5 minutes

Cooking Time: 10 minutes

Servings: 2

Ingredients:

For Chaffle:

- Egg: 2
- Cream Cheese: 2 oz. softened
- Almond flour: 2 tbsp.
- Vanilla Extract: 2 tsp.
- Cinnamon: 2 tsp.
- Vanilla extract: 2 tsp.
- Splenda: 2 tbsp.

For Icing:

- Cream cheese: 2 oz. softened
- Splenda: 2 tbsp.
- Vanilla: 1 tsp.
- Butter: 2 tbsp. unsalted butter

For Cinnamon Drizzle:

- Splenda: 2 tbsp.
- Butter: 1 tbsp.
- Cinnamon: 2 tsp.

Directions:

1. Preheat the waffle maker

2. Grease it lightly

3. Mix all the chaffle ingredients together

4. Pour the mixture to the waffle maker

5. Cooking for around 4 minutes or till chaffles become crispy

6. Keep them aside when done

7. In a small bowl, mix the ingredients of icing and cinnamon drizzle

8. Heat it in a microwave for about 10 seconds to gain a soft uniformity

9. Whirl on cooled chaffles and enjoy!

Nutrition: Calories: 323; Total Fat: 27g; Carbs: 8g; Net Carbs: 3g;

Fiber: 5g; Protein: 15g

Raspberries Chaffle

Preparation time: 15 minutes

Cooking Time: 15 Minutes

Servings: 1

Ingredients:

- 1 egg white
- 1/4 cup jack cheese, shredded
- 1/4 cup cheddar cheese, shredded
- 1 tsp. coconut flour
- 1/4 tsp. baking powder
- 1/2 tsp. stevia

For Topping

- 4 oz. raspberries
- 2 tbsps. coconut flour
- 2 oz. unsweetened raspberry sauce

Directions:

1. Switch on your round Waffle Maker and grease it with cooking spray once it is hot.
2. Mix together all chaffle ingredients in a bowl and combine with a fork.
3. Pour chaffle batter in a preheated maker and close the lid.
4. Roll the taco chaffle around using a kitchen roller, set it aside and allow it to set for a few minutes.

5. Once the taco chaffle is set, remove from the roller.
6. Dip raspberries in sauce and arrange on taco chaffle.
7. Drizzle coconut flour on top.
8. Enjoy raspberries taco chaffle with keto coffee.

Nutrition: Calories: 386; Total Fat: 37g; Carbs: 13g; Net Carbs: 8g;

Fiber: 5g; Protein: 5g

Garlic and Parsley Chaffles

Preparation time: 10 minutes

Cooking Time: 5 Minutes

Servings: 1

Ingredients:

- 1 large egg
- 1/4 cup cheese Mozzarella
- 1 tsp. coconut flour
- ¼ tsp. baking powder
- ½ tsp. garlic powder
- 1 tbsp. minute sced parsley

For Serving

- 1 Poach egg
- 4 oz. smoked salmon

Directions:

1. Switch on your Dash waffle maker and let it preheat.
2. Grease waffle maker with cooking spray.
3. Mix together egg, mozzarella, coconut flour, and baking powder, and garlic powder, parsley to a mixing bowl until combined well.
4. Pour batter in circle chaffle maker.
5. Close the lid.

6. Cooking for about 2-3 minutes or until the chaffles is cooked.
7. Serve with smoked salmon and poached egg.
8. Enjoy!

Nutrition: Calories: 757; Total Fat: 38g; Carbs: 17g; Net Carbs: 11g;

Fiber: 6g; Protein: 29g

Scrambled Eggs and A Spring Onion Chaffle

Preparation time: 10 minutes

Cooking Time: 7–9 Minutes

Servings: 4

Ingredients:

Batter

- 4 eggs
- 2 cups grated Mozzarella cheese
- 2 spring onions, finely chopped
- Salt and pepper to taste
- ½ teaspoon dried garlic powder
- 2 tablespoons almond flour
- 2 tablespoons coconut flour

Other

- 2 tablespoons butter for brushing the waffle maker
- 6-8 eggs
- Salt and pepper
- 1 teaspoon Italian spice mix
- 1 tablespoon olive oil
- 1 tablespoon freshly chopped parsley

Directions:

1. Preheat the waffle maker.
2. Crack the eggs into a bowl and add the grated cheese.
3. Mix until just combined, then add the chopped spring onions and season with salt and pepper and dried garlic powder.
4. Stir in the almond flour and mix until everything is combined.
5. Brush the heated waffle maker with butter and add a few tablespoons of the batter.
6. Close the lid and cooking for about 7–8 minutes depending on your waffle maker.
7. While the chaffles are cooking, the scrambled eggs by whisking the eggs in a bowl until frothy, about 2 minutes. Season with salt and black pepper to taste and add the Italian spice mix. Whisk to blend in the spices.
8. Warm the oil in a non-stick pan over medium heat.
9. Pour the eggs in the pan and cooking until eggs are set to your liking.
10. Serve each chaffle and top with some scrambled eggs. Top with freshly chopped parsley.

Nutrition: Calories: 165; Total Fat: 15g; Carbs: 4g; Net Carbs: 2g;

Fiber: 2g; Protein: 6g

Egg and A Cheddar Cheese Chaffle

Preparation time: 10 minutes

Cooking Time: 7–9 Minutes

Servings: 4

Ingredients:

Batter

- 4 eggs
- 2 cups shredded white cheddar cheese
- Salt and pepper to taste

Other

- 2 tablespoons butter for brushing the waffle maker
- 4 large eggs
- 2 tablespoons olive oil

Directions:

1. Preheat the waffle maker.
2. Crack the eggs into a bowl and whisk them with a fork.
3. Stir in the grated cheddar cheese and season with salt and pepper.
4. Brush the heated waffle maker with butter and add a few tablespoons of the batter.
5. Close the lid and cooking for about 7–8 minutes depending on your waffle maker.

6. While chaffles are cooking, cooking the eggs.

7. Warm the oil in a large non-stick pan that has a lid over medium-low heat for 2-3 minutes

8. Crack an egg in a small ramekin and gently add it to the pan. Repeat the same way for the other 3 eggs.

9. Cover and let cooking for 2 to 2 ½ minutes for set eggs but with runny yolks.

10. Remove from heat.

11. To serve, place a chaffle on each plate and top with an egg. Season with salt and black pepper to taste.

Nutrition: Calories: 74; Total Fat: 7g; Carbs: 1g; Net Carbs: 0g;

Fiber: 0g; Protein: 3g

Avocado Chaffle Toast

Preparation time: 15 minutes

Cooking Time: 10 Minutes

Servings: 3

Ingredients:

- 4 tbsps. avocado mash
- 1/2 tsp. lemon juice
- 1/8 tsp. salt
- 1/8 tsp. black pepper
- 2 eggs
- 1/2 cup shredded cheese

For serving

- 3 eggs
- ½ avocado thinly sliced
- 1 tomato, sliced

Directions:

1. Mash avocado mash with lemon juice, salt, and black pepper in mixing bowl, until well combined.
2. In a small bowl beat egg and pour eggs in avocado mixture and mix well.
3. Switch on Waffle Maker to pre-heat.
4. Pour 1/8 of shredded cheese in a waffle maker and then pour ½ of egg and avocado mixture and then 1/8 shredded cheese.

5. Close the lid and cooking chaffles for about 3 - 4 minutes.
6. Repeat with the remaining mixture.
7. Meanwhile, fry eggs in a pan for about 1-2 minutes.
8. For serving, arrange fried egg on chaffle toast with avocado slice and tomatoes.
9. Sprinkle salt and pepper on top and enjoy!

Nutrition: Calories: 323; Total Fat: 24g; Carbs: 6g; Net Carbs: 4g; Fiber: 3g; Protein: 23g

Chili Chaffle

Preparation time: 10 minutes

Cooking Time: 7–9 Minutes

Servings: 4

Ingredients:

Batter

- 4 eggs
- ½ cup grated parmesan cheese
- 1½ cups grated yellow cheddar cheese
- 1 hot red chili pepper
- Salt and pepper to taste
- ½ teaspoon dried garlic powder
- 1 teaspoon dried basil
- 2 tablespoons almond flour

Other

- 2 tablespoons olive oil for brushing the waffle maker

Directions:

1. Preheat the waffle maker.
2. Crack the eggs into a bowl and add the grated parmesan and cheddar cheese.
3. Mix until just combined and add the chopped chili pepper. Season with salt and pepper, dried garlic powder and dried basil. Stir in the almond flour.

4. Mix until everything is combined.

5. Brush the heated waffle maker with olive oil and add a few tablespoons of the batter.

6. Close the lid and cooking for about 7–8 minutes depending on your waffle maker.

Nutrition: Calories: 859; Total Fat: 73g; Carbs: 8g; Net Carbs: 8g;

Fiber: 0g; Protein: 41g

Simple Savory Chaffle

Preparation time: 10 minutes

Cooking Time: 7–9 Minutes

Servings: 4

Ingredients:

Batter

- 4 eggs
- 1 cup grated Mozzarella cheese
- 1 cup grated provolone cheese
- ½ cup almond flour
- 2 tablespoons coconut flour
- 2½ teaspoons baking powder
- Salt and pepper to taste

Other

- 2 tablespoons butter to brush the waffle maker

Directions:

1. Preheat the waffle maker.
2. Add the grated Mozzarella and provolone cheese to a bowl and mix.
3. Add the almond and coconut flour and baking powder and season with salt and pepper.
4. Mix with a wire whisk and crack in the eggs.
5. Stir everything together until batter forms.

6. Brush the heated waffle maker with butter and add a few tablespoons of the batter.

7. Close the lid and cooking for about 8 minutes depending on your waffle maker.

8. Serve and enjoy.

Nutrition: Calories: 248; Total Fat: 18g; Carbs: 11g; Net Carbs: 7g;

Fiber: 5g; Protein: 14g

Pizza Chaffles

Preparation time: 10 minutes

Cooking Time: 7–9 Minutes

Servings: 4

Ingredients:

Batter

- 4 eggs
- 1½ cups grated Mozzarella cheese
- ½ cup grated parmesan cheese
- 2 tablespoons tomato sauce
- ¼ cup almond flour
- 1½ teaspoons baking powder
- Salt and pepper to taste
- 1 teaspoon dried oregano
- ¼ cup sliced salami

Other

- 2 tablespoons olive oil for brushing the waffle maker
- ¼ cup tomato sauce for serving

Directions:

1. Preheat the waffle maker.
2. Add the grated Mozzarella and grated parmesan to a bowl and mix.

3. Add the almond flour and baking powder and season with salt and pepper and dried oregano.
4. Mix with a wooden spoon or wire whisk and crack in the eggs.
5. Stir everything together until batter forms.
6. Stir in the chopped salami.
7. Brush the heated waffle maker with olive oil and add a few tablespoons of the batter.
8. Close the lid and cooking for about 7–minutes depending on your waffle maker.
9. Serve with extra tomato sauce on top and enjoy.

Nutrition: Calories: 583; Total Fat: 54g; Carbs: 7g; Net Carbs: 7g;

Fiber: 0g; Protein: 19g

Bacon Chaffle

Preparation time: 10 minutes

Cooking Time: 7–9 Minutes

Servings: 4

Ingredients:

Batter

- 4 eggs
- 2 cups shredded Mozzarella
- 2 ounces finely chopped bacon
- Salt and pepper to taste
- 1 teaspoon dried oregano

Other

- 2 tablespoons olive oil for brushing the waffle maker

Directions:

1. Preheat the waffle maker.
2. Crack the eggs into a bowl and add the grated Mozzarella cheese.
3. Mix until just combined and stir in the chopped bacon.
4. Season with salt and pepper and dried oregano.
5. Brush the heated waffle maker with olive oil and add a few tablespoons of the batter.

6. Close the lid and cooking for about 7–8 minutes depending on your waffle maker.

Nutrition: Calories: 164; Total Fat: 13g; Carbs: 1g; Net Carbs: 1g;

Fiber: 0g; Protein: 9g

Simple Chaffle

Preparation time: 10 minutes

Cooking Time: 5 minutes

Servings: 4

Ingredients:

- 1 cup egg whites
- 1 cup cheddar cheese, shredded
- ¼ cup almond flour
- ¼ cup heavy cream
- 4 oz. raspberries
- 4 oz. strawberries.
- 1 oz. keto chocolate flakes
- 1 oz. feta cheese.

Directions:

1. Preheat your square waffle maker and grease with cooking spray.
2. Beat egg white in a small bowl with flour.
3. Add shredded cheese to the egg whites and flour mixture and mix well.
4. Add cream and cheese to the egg mixture.
5. Pour Chaffles batter in a waffle maker and close the lid.
6. Cooking chaffles for about 4 minutes until crispy and brown.

7. Carefully remove chaffles from the maker.

8. Serve with berries, cheese, and chocolate on top.

9. Enjoy!

Nutrition: Calories: 254; Total Fat: 19g; Carbs: 11g; Net Carbs: 7g;

Fiber: 4g; Protein: 11g

Chaffles Breakfast Bowl

Preparation Time: 15 min

Cooking Time: 5 min

Servings: 2

Ingredients:

- 1 egg
- 1/2 cup cheddar cheese shredded
- pinch of Italian seasoning
- 1 tbsp. pizza sauce
- 1/2 avocado sliced
- 2 eggs boiled
- 1 tomato, halves
- 4 oz. fresh spinach leaves

Directions:

1. Preheat your waffle maker and grease with cooking spray.
2. Crack an egg in a small bowl and beat with Italian seasoning and pizza sauce.
3. Add shredded cheese to the egg and spices mixture.
4. Pour 1 tbsp. shredded cheese in a waffle maker and cooking for 30 sec.
5. Pour Chaffles batter in the waffle maker and close the lid.
6. Cooking chaffles for about 4 minutes until crispy and brown.

7. Carefully remove chaffles from the maker.

8. Serve on the bed of spinach with boil egg, avocado slice, and tomatoes.

9. Enjoy!

Nutrition: Calories: 549; Total Fat: 49g; Carbs: 16g; Net Carbs: 11g:

Fiber: 5g; Protein: 16g

Crispy Chaffles With Sausage

Preparation Time: 15 min

Cooking Time: 10 min

Servings: 2

Ingredients

- 1/2 cup cheddar cheese
- 1/2 tsp. baking powder
- 1/4 cup egg whites
- 2 tsp. pumpkin spice
- 1 egg, whole
- 2 chicken sausage
- 2 slice bacon
- salt and pepper to taste
- 1 tsp. avocado oil

Directions

1. Mix together all ingredients in a bowl.
2. Allow batter to sit while waffle iron warms.
3. Spray waffle iron with nonstick spray.
4. Pour batter in the waffle maker and cooking according to the directions of the manufacturer.
5. Meanwhile, heat oil in a pan and fry the egg, according to your choice and transfer it to a plate.
6. In the same pan, fry bacon slice and sausage on medium heat for about 2-3 minutes until cooked.
7. Once chaffles are cooked thoroughly, remove them from the maker.

8. Serve with fried egg, bacon slice, sausages and enjoy!

Nutrition: Calories: 204 kcal Total Fat: 11g Total Carbs: 4.2g Protein: 1.5g

Mini Breakfast Chaffles

Preparation Time: 30 min

Cooking Time: 15 min

Servings: 3

Ingredients:

- 6 tsp. coconut flour
- 1 tsp. stevia
- 1/4 tsp. baking powder
- 2 eggs
- 3 oz. cream cheese
- 1/2. tsp. vanilla extract
- 1 egg
- 6 slice bacon
- 2 oz. Raspberries for topping
- 2 oz. Blueberries for topping
- 2 oz. Strawberries for topping

Directions:

1. Heat up your square waffle maker and grease with cooking spray.
2. Mix together coconut flour, stevia, egg, baking powder, cheese and vanilla in mixing bowl.
3. Pour ½ of chaffles mixture in a waffle maker.
4. Close the lid and cooking the chaffles for about 3-5 minutes.

5. Meanwhile, fry bacon slices in pan on medium heat for about 2-3 minutes until cooked and transfer them to plate.

6. In the same pan, fry eggs one by one in the leftover grease of bacon.

7. Once chaffles are cooked, carefully transfer them to plate.

8. Serve with fried eggs and bacon slice and berries on top.

9. Enjoy!

Nutrition: Calories: 665 Net Carbs: 6.2g Fat: 54g Protein: 32g

Crispy Chaffles With Egg and Asparagus

Preparation Time: 15 min

Cooking Time: 10 min

Servings: 1

Ingredients:

- 1 egg
- 1/4 cup cheddar cheese
- 2 tbsps. almond flour
- ½ tsp. baking powder
- 1 egg
- 4-5 stalks asparagus
- 1 tsp. avocado oil

Directions:

1. Preheat waffle maker to medium-high heat.
2. Whisk together egg, Mozzarella cheese, almond flour, and baking powder
3. Pour chaffles mixture into the center of the waffle iron. Close the waffle maker and let cooking for 3-5 minutes or until waffle is golden brown and set.
4. Remove chaffles from the waffle maker and serve.
5. Meanwhile, heat oil in a nonstick pan.
6. Once the pan is hot, fry asparagus for about 4-5 minutes until golden brown.
7. Poach the egg in boil water for about 2-3 minutes.

8. Once chaffles are cooked, remove from the maker.

9. Serve chaffles with the poached egg and asparagus.

Nutrition: Calories: 287 kcal Total Fat: 19g Total Carbs: 6.5g Protein: 6.8g

Coconut Chaffles

Preparation Time: 10 minutes

Cooking Time: 5 minutes

Servings: 2

Ingredients:

- 1 egg
- 1 oz. cream cheese,
- 1 oz. cheddar cheese
- 2 tbsps. coconut flour
- 1 tsp. stevia
- 1 tbsp. coconut oil, melted
- 1/2 tsp. coconut extract
- 2 eggs, soft boil for serving

Directions:

1. Heat your waffle maker and grease with cooking spray.
2. Mix together all chaffles ingredients in a bowl.
3. Pour chaffle batter in a preheated waffle maker.
4. Close the lid.
5. Cooking chaffles for about 2-3 minutes until golden brown.
6. Serve with boil egg and enjoy

Nutrition: Calories: 331 kcal Protein: 11.84 g Fat: 30.92 g Carbohydrates: 1.06g

Cajun & Feta Chaffles

Preparation Time: 30 min

Cooking Time: 10 min

Servings: 1

Ingredients

- 1 egg white
- 1/4 cup shredded Mozzarella cheese
- 2 tbsps. almond flour
- 1 tsp. Cajun Seasoning

For Serving

- 1 egg
- 4 oz. feta cheese
- 1 tomato, sliced

Directions

1. Whisk together egg, cheese, and seasoning in a bowl.
2. Switch on and grease waffle maker with cooking spray.
3. Pour batter in a preheated waffle maker.
4. Cooking chaffles for about 2-3 minutes until the chaffle is cooked through.
5. Meanwhile, fry the egg in a non-stick pan for about 1-2 minutes.
6. For serving set fried egg on chaffles with feta cheese and tomatoes slice.

Nutrition: Calorie Count: 103 Protein: 7 g Fat: 9 g Carbohydrates: 1 g

LUNCH CHAFFLE RECIPES

Chicken Bites with Chaffles

Preparation time: 10 minutes

Cooking Time: 10 minutes

Servings: 2

Ingredients:

- 1 chicken breasts cut into 2 x2 inch chunks
- 1 egg, whisked
- 1/4 cup almond flour
- 2 tbsps. onion powder
- 2 tbsps. garlic powder
- 1 tsp. dried oregano
- 1 tsp. paprika powder
- 1 tsp. salt
- 1/2 tsp. black pepper
- 2 tbsps. avocado oil

Directions:

1. Add all the dry ingredients together into a large bowl. Mix well.
2. Place the eggs into a separate bowl.

3. Dip each chicken piece into the egg and then into the dry ingredients.

4. Heat oil in 10-inch skillet, add oil.

5. Once avocado oil is hot, place the coated chicken nuggets onto a skillet and cook for 6-8 minutes Utes until cooked and golden brown.

6. Serve with chaffles and raspberries.

7. Enjoy!

Nutrition: Total Calories 401 kcal Fats 219 g Protein 32.35 g Nectars 1.46 g Fiber 3 g

Fish and Chaffle Bites

Preparation time: 10 minutes

Cooking Time: 15 minutes

Servings: 2

Ingredients:

- 1 lb. cod fillets, sliced into 4 slices
- 1 tsp. sea salt
- 1 tsp. garlic powder
- 1 egg, whisked
- 1 cup almond flour
- 2 tbsp. avocado oil

Chaffle Ingredients:

- 2 eggs
- 1/2 cup cheddar cheese
- 2 tbsps. almond flour
- ½ tsp. Italian seasoning

Directions:

1. Mix together chaffle ingredients in a bowl and make 4 squares
2. Put the chaffles in a preheated chaffle maker.
3. Mix together the salt, pepper, and garlic powder in a mixing bowl. Toss the cod cubes in this mixture and let sit for 10 minutes Utes.

4. Then dip each cod slice into the egg mixture and then into the almond flour.
5. Heat oil in skillet and fish cubes for about 2-3 minutes Utes, until cooked and browned
6. Serve on chaffles and enjoy!

Nutrition: Protein: 38% 121 kcal Fat: 59% 189 kcal Carbohydrates: 3% 11 kcal

Grill Pork Chaffle Sandwich

Preparation time: 10 minutes

Cooking Time: 15 Minutes

Servings:2

Ingredients:

- 1/2 cup mozzarella, shredded
- 1 egg
- I pinch garlic powder

Pork Patty

- 1/2 cup pork, minutes
- 1 tbsp. green onion, diced
- 1/2 tsp Italian seasoning
- Lettuce leaves

Directions:

1. Preheat the square waffle maker and grease with
2. Mix together egg, cheese and garlic powder in a small mixing bowl.
3. Pour batter in a preheated waffle maker and close the lid.
4. Make 2 chaffles from this batter.
5. Cook chaffles for about 2-3 minutes Utes until cooked through.
6. Meanwhile, mix together pork patty ingredients in a bowl and make 1 large patty.

7. Grill pork patty in a preheated grill for about 3-4 minutes Utes per side until cooked through.

8. Arrange pork patty between two chaffles with lettuce leaves. Cut sandwich to make a triangular sandwich.

9. Enjoy!

Nutrition: Protein: 48% 85 kcal Fat: 48% 86 kcal Carbohydrates: 4% 7 kcal

Chaffles & Chicken Lunch Plate

Preparation time: 10 minutes

Cooking Time: 15 Minutes

Servings:2

Ingredients:

- 1 large egg
- 1/2 cup jack cheese, shredded
- 1 pinch salt

For Serving

- 1 chicken leg
- salt
- pepper
- 1 tsp. garlic, minutes
- 1 egg
- 1 tsp avocado oil

Directions:

1. Heat your square waffle maker and grease with cooking spray.
2. Pour Chaffle batter into the skillet and cook for about 3 minutes Utes.
3. Meanwhile, heat oil in a pan, over medium heat.
4. Once the oil is hot, add chicken thigh and garlic then, cook for about 5 minutes Utes. Flip and cook for another 3-4 minutes.

63

5. Season with salt and pepper and give them a good mix.
6. Transfer cooked thigh to plate.
7. Fry the egg in the same pan for about 1-2 minutes Utes according to your choice.
8. Once chaffles are cooked, serve with fried egg and chicken thigh.
9. Enjoy!

Nutrition: Protein: 31% 138 kcal Fat: 66% 292 kcal Carbohydrates: 2% kcal

Chaffle Egg Sandwich

Preparation time: 10 minutes

Cooking Time: 10 Minutes

Servings:2

Ingredients:

- 2 keto chaffle
- 2 slice cheddar cheese
- 1 egg simple omelet

Directions:

1. Prepare your oven on 4000 F.
2. Arrange egg omelet and cheese slice between chaffles.
3. Bake in the preheated oven for about 4-5 minutes Utes until cheese is melted.
4. Once the cheese is melted, remove from the oven.
5. Serve and enjoy!

Nutrition: Protein: 29% 144 kcal Fat: % 337 kcal Carbohydrates: 3% 14 kcal

Chaffle Minutes Sandwich

Preparation time: 10 minutes

Cooking Time: 10 Minutes

Servings:2

Ingredients:

- 1 large egg
- 1/8 cup almond flour
- 1/2 tsp. garlic powder
- 3/4 tsp. baking powder
- 1/2 cup shredded cheese

Sandwich Filling

- 2 slices deli ham
- 2 slices tomatoes
- 1 slice cheddar cheese

Directions:

1. Grease your square waffle maker and preheat it on medium heat.
2. Mix together chaffle ingredients in a mixing bowl until well combined.
3. Pour batter into a square waffle and make two chaffles.
4. Once chaffles are cooked, remove from the maker.

5. For a sandwich, arrange deli ham, tomato slice and cheddar cheese between two chaffles.

6. Cut sandwich from the center.

7. Serve and enjoy!

Nutrition: Protein: 29% 70 kcal Fat: 66% 159 kcal Carbohydrates: 4% 10 kcal

Chaffle Cheese Sandwich

Preparation time: 10 minutes

Cooking Time: 10 Minutes

Servings: 1

Ingredients:

- 2 square keto chaffle
- 2 slice cheddar cheese
- 2 lettuce leaves

Directions:

1. Prepare your oven on 4000 F.
2. Arrange lettuce leave and cheese slice between chaffles.
3. Bake in the preheated oven for about 4-5 minutes Utes until cheese is melted.
4. Once the cheese is melted, remove from the oven.
5. Serve and enjoy!

Nutrition: Protein: 28% kcal Fat: 69% 149 kcal Carbohydrates: 3% 6 kcal

Chicken Zinger Chaffle

Preparation time: 10 minutes

Cooking Time: 15 Minutes

Servings:2

Ingredients:

- 1 chicken breast, cut into 2 pieces
- 1/2 cup coconut flour
- 1/4 cup finely grated Parmesan
- 1 tsp. paprika
- 1/2 tsp. garlic powder
- 1/2 tsp. onion powder
- 1 tsp. salt& pepper
- 1 egg beaten
- Avocado oil for frying
- Lettuce leaves
- BBQ sauce

Chaffle Ingredients:

- 4 oz. cheese
- 2 whole eggs
- 2 oz. almond flour
- 1/4 cup almond flour
- 1 tsp baking powder

Directions:

1. Mix together chaffle ingredients in a bowl.

---

2. Pour the chaffle batter in preheated greased square chaffle maker.

3. Cook chaffles for about 2-minutesutes until cooked through.

4. Make square chaffles from this batter.

5. Meanwhile mix together coconut flour, parmesan, paprika, garlic powder, onion powder salt and pepper in a bowl.

6. Dip chicken first in coconut flour mixture then in beaten egg.

7. Heat avocado oil in a skillet and cook chicken from both sides. until lightly brown and cooked

8. Set chicken zinger between two chaffles with lettuce and BBQ sauce.

9. Enjoy!

Nutrition: Protein: 30% 219 kcal Fat: 60% 435 kcal Carbohydrates: 9% 66 kcal

Double Chicken Chaffles

Preparation time: 10 minutes

Cooking Time: 5 Minutes

Servings:2

Ingredients:

- 1/2 cup boil shredded chicken
- 1/4 cup cheddar cheese
- 1/8 cup parmesan cheese
- 1 egg
- 1 tsp. Italian seasoning
- 1/8 tsp. garlic powder
- 1 tsp. cream cheese

Directions:

1. Preheat the Belgian waffle maker.
2. Mix together in chaffle ingredients in a bowl and mix together.
3. Sprinkle 1 tbsp. of cheese in a waffle maker and pour in chaffle batter.
4. Pour 1 tbsp. of cheese over batter and close the lid.
5. Cook chaffles for about 4 to minutes Utes.
6. Serve with a chicken zinger and enjoy the double chicken flavor.

Nutrition: Protein: 30% 60 kcal Fat: 65% 129 kcal Carbohydrates: 5% 9 kcal

Chaffles With Topping

Preparation time: 10 minutes

Cooking Time: 10 Minutes

Servings:2

Ingredients:

- 1 large egg
- 1 tbsp. almond flour
- 1 tbsp. full-fat Greek yogurt
- 1/8 tsp baking powder
- 1/4 cup shredded Swiss cheese

Topping

- 4oz. grill prawns
- 4 oz. steamed cauliflower mash
- 1/2 zucchini sliced
- 3 lettuce leaves
- 1 tomato, sliced
- 1 tbsp. flax seeds

Directions:

1. Make 3 chaffles with the given chaffles ingredients.
2. For serving, arrange lettuce leaves on each chaffle.
3. Top with zucchini slice, grill prawns, cauliflower mash and a tomato slice.

4. Drizzle flax seeds on top.

5. Serve and enjoy!

Nutrition: Protein: 45% 71 kcal Fat: 47% 75 kcal Carbohydrates: 8% 12 kcal

Chaffle With Cheese & Bacon

Preparation time: 10 minutes

Cooking Time: 15 Minutes

Servings:2

Ingredients:

- 1 egg
- 1/2 cup cheddar cheese, shredded
- 1 tbsp. parmesan cheese
- 3/4 tsp coconut flour
- 1/4 tsp baking powder
- 1/8 tsp Italian Seasoning
- pinch of salt
- 1/4 tsp garlic powder

For Topping

- 1 bacon sliced, cooked and chopped
- 1/2 cup mozzarella cheese, shredded
- 1/4 tsp parsley, chopped

Directions:

1. Preheat oven to 400 degrees.
2. Switch on your minutes waffle maker and grease with cooking spray.
3. Mix together chaffle ingredients in a mixing bowl until combined.

4. Spoon half of the batter in the center of the waffle maker and close the lid. Cook chaffles for about 3-minutesutes until cooked.
5. Carefully remove chaffles from the maker.
6. Arrange chaffles in a greased baking tray.
7. Top with mozzarella cheese, chopped bacon and parsley.
8. And bake in the oven for 4 -5 minutes Utes.
9. Once the cheese is melted, remove from the oven.
10. Serve and enjoy!

Nutrition: Protein: 28% 90 kcal Fat: 69% 222 kcal Carbohydrates: 3% kcal

Grill Beefsteak and Chaffle

Preparation time: 10 minutes

Cooking Time: 10 Minutes

Servings: 1

Ingredients:

- 1 beefsteak rib eye
- 1 tsp salt
- 1 tsp pepper
- 1 tbsp. lime juice
- 1 tsp garlic

Directions:

1. Prepare your grill for direct heat.
2. Mix together all spices and rub over beefsteak evenly.
3. Place the beef on the grill rack over medium heat.
4. Cover and cook steak for about6 to 8 minutes Utes. Flip and cook for another 5 minutes Utes until cooked through.
5. Serve with keto simple chaffle and enjoy!

Nutrition: Protein: 51% 274 kcal Fat: 45% 243 kcal Carbohydrates: 4% 22 kcal

Cauliflower Chaffles And Tomatoes

Preparation time: 10 minutes

Cooking Time: 15 Minutes

Servings:2

Ingredients:

- 1/2 cup cauliflower
- 1/4 tsp. garlic powder
- 1/4 tsp. black pepper
- 1/4 tsp. Salt
- 1/2 cup shredded cheddar cheese
- 1 egg

For Topping

- 1 lettuce leave
- 1 tomato sliced
- 4 oz. cauliflower steamed, mashed
- 1 tsp sesame seeds

Directions:

1. Add all chaffle ingredients into a blender and mix well.
2. Sprinkle 1/8 shredded cheese on the waffle maker and pour cauliflower mixture in a preheated waffle maker and sprinkle the rest of the cheese over it.

---

3. Cook chaffles for about 4-5 minutes Utes until cooked
4. For serving, lay lettuce leaves over chaffle top with steamed cauliflower and tomato.
5. Drizzle sesame seeds on top.
6. Enjoy!

Nutrition: Protein: 25% 49 kcal Fat: 65% 128 kcal Carbohydrates: 10% 21 kcal

Rosemary Pork Chops in Chaffles

Preparation time: 10 minutes

Cooking Time:15 Minutes

Servings: 2

Ingredients:

- 4 eggs
- 2 cups grated mozzarella cheese
- Salt and pepper to taste
- Pinch of nutmeg
- 2 tablespoons sour cream
- 6 tablespoons almond flour
- 2 teaspoons baking powder
- Pork chops
- 2 tablespoons olive oil
- 1 pound pork chops
- Salt and pepper to taste
- 1 teaspoon freshly chopped rosemary
- Other
- 2 tablespoons cooking spray to brush the waffle maker
- 2 tablespoons freshly chopped basil for decoration

Directions:

1. Preheat the waffle maker.

---

2. Add the eggs, mozzarella cheese, salt and pepper, nutmeg, sour cream, almond flour and baking powder to a bowl.

3. Mix until combined.

4. Brush the heated waffle maker with cooking spray and add a few tablespoons of the batter.

5. Close the lid and cook for about 7 minutes depending on your waffle maker.

6. Meanwhile, heat the butter in a nonstick grill pan and season the pork chops with salt and pepper and freshly chopped rosemary.

7. Cook the pork chops for about 4–5 minutes on each side.

8. Serve each chaffle with a pork chop and sprinkle some freshly chopped basil on top.

Nutrition: Calories 666, fat 55.2 g, carbs 4.8 g, sugar 0.4 g, Protein 37.5 g, sodium 235 mg

Classic Beef Chaffle

Preparation time: 10 minutes

Cooking Time: 10 Minutes

Servings: 2

Ingredients:

Batter

- ½ pound ground beef
- 4 eggs
- 4 ounces cream cheese
- 1 cup grated mozzarella cheese
- Salt and pepper to taste
- 1 clove garlic, minced
- ½ teaspoon freshly chopped rosemary

Other

- 2 tablespoons butter to brush the waffle maker
- ¼ cup sour cream
- 2 tablespoons freshly chopped parsley for garnish

Directions:

1. Preheat the waffle maker.
2. Add the ground beef, eggs, cream cheese, grated mozzarella cheese, salt and pepper, minced garlic and freshly chopped rosemary to a bowl.
3. Brush the heated waffle maker with butter and add a few tablespoons of the batter.

4. Close the lid and cook for about 8–10 minutes depending on your waffle maker.

5. Serve each chaffle with a tablespoon of sour cream and freshly chopped parsley on top.

6. Serve and enjoy.

Nutrition: Calories 368, fat 24 g, carbs 2.1 g, sugar 0.4 g, Protein 27.4 g, sodium 291 mg

Beef and Tomato Chaffle

Preparation time: 10 minutes

Cooking Time:15 Minutes

Servings: 2

Ingredients:

Batter

- 4 eggs
- ¼ cup cream cheese
- 1 cup grated mozzarella cheese
- Salt and pepper to taste
- ¼ cup almond flour
- 1 teaspoon freshly chopped dill

Beef

- 1 pound beef loin
- Salt and pepper to taste
- 1 tablespoon balsamic vinegar
- 2 tablespoons olive oil
- 1 teaspoon freshly chopped rosemary

Other

- 2 tablespoons cooking spray to brush the waffle maker
- 4 tomato slices for serving

Directions:

1. Preheat the waffle maker.

---

2. Add the eggs, cream cheese, grated mozzarella cheese, salt and pepper, almond flour and freshly chopped dill to a bowl.

3. Mix until combined and batter forms.

4. Brush the heated waffle maker with cooking spray and add a few tablespoons of the batter.

5. Close the lid and cook for about 8–10 minutes depending on your waffle maker.

6. Meanwhile, heat the olive oil in a nonstick frying pan and season the beef loin with salt and pepper and freshly chopped rosemary.

7. Cook the beef on each side for about 5 minutes and drizzle with some balsamic vinegar.

8. Serve each chaffle with a slice of tomato and cooked beef loin slices.

Nutrition: Calories 4, fat 35.8 g, carbs 3.3 g, sugar 0.8 g, Protein 40.3 g, sodium 200 mg

Classic Ground Pork Chaffle

Preparation time: 10 minutes

Cooking Time:15 Minutes

Servings: 2

Ingredients:

- ½ pound ground pork
- 3 eggs
- ½ cup grated mozzarella cheese
- Salt and pepper to taste
- 1 clove garlic, minced
- 1 teaspoon dried oregano
- Other
- 2 tablespoons butter to brush the waffle maker
- 2 tablespoons freshly chopped parsley for garnish

Directions:

1. Preheat the waffle maker.
2. Add the ground pork, eggs, mozzarella cheese, salt and pepper, minced garlic and dried oregano to a bowl.
3. Mix until combined.
4. Brush the heated waffle maker with butter and add a few tablespoons of the batter.
5. Close the lid and cook for about 7–8 minutes depending on your waffle maker.

6. Serve with freshly chopped parsley.

Nutrition: Calories 192, fat 11.g, carbs 1 g, sugar 0.3 g, Protein 20.2 g, sodium 142 mg

Spicy Jalapeno Popper Chaffles

Preparation time: 10 mins

Cooking time: 10 mins

Servings: 1

Ingredients: for the chaffles:

- 1 egg
- 1 oz cream cheese, softened
- 1 cup cheddar cheese, shredded
- For the toppings:
- 2 tbsp bacon bits
- 1/2 tbsp jalapenos

Directions:

1. Turn on the waffle maker. Preheat for up to 5 minutes.
2. Mix the chaffle Ingredients.
3. Pour the batter onto the waffle maker.
4. Cook the batter for 3-4 minutes until it's brown and crispy.
5. Remove the chaffle and repeat steps until all remaining batter have been used up.
6. Sprinkle bacon bits and a few jalapeno slices as toppings.

Nutrition: calories: 231 carbohydrate: 2g fat: 18g protein: 13g

Eggnog Chaffles

Preparation time: 15 minutes

Cooking time: 10 minutes

Servings: 1

Ingredients:

- 1 egg, separated
- 1 egg yolk
- 1/2 cup mozzarella cheese Shredded
- 1/2 tsp spiced rum
- 1 tsp vanilla extract
- 1/4 tsp nutmeg, dried
- A dash of cinnamon
- 1 tsp coconut flour
- For the icing:
- 2 tbsp cream cheese
- 1 tbsp powdered sweetener
- 2 tsp rum or rum extract

Directions:

1. Preheat the mini waffle maker.
2. Mix egg yolk in a small bowl until smooth.
3. Add in the sweetener and mix until the powder is completely dissolved.
4. Add the coconut flour, cinnamon, and nutmeg. Mix well.

5. In another bowl, mix rum, egg white, and vanilla. Whisk until well combined.

6. Throw in the yolk mixture with the egg white mixture. You should be able to form a thin batter.

7. Add the mozzarella cheese and combine with the mixture.

8. Separate the batter into two batches. Put 1/2 of the batter into the waffle maker and let it cook for 6 minutes until it's solid.

9. Repeat until you've used up the remaining batter.

10. In a separate bowl, mix all the icing Ingredients.

11. Top the cooked chaffles with the icing, or you can use this as a dip.

Nutrition: calories: 266 carbohydrates: 2g fat: 23g protein: 13g

Cheddar Jalapeno Chaffles

Preparation time: 15 minutes

Cooking time: 10 minutes

Servings: 1

Ingredients:

- 1 egg
- 1/2 cup cheddar cheese shredded
- 1 tbsp almond flour
- 1 tbsp jalapenos
- 1 tbsp olive oil

Directions:

1. Preheat the waffle maker.
2. While waiting for the waffle maker to heat up, mix jalapeno, egg, cheese, and almond flour in a small mixing bowl.
3. Lightly grease the waffle maker with olive oil.
4. In the center of the waffle maker, carefully pour the chaffle batter. Spread the mixture evenly toward the edges.
5. Close the waffle maker lid and wait for 3-4 minutes for the mixture to cook. For an even crispier texture, wait for another 1-2 minutes.
6. Remove the chaffle. Let it cool before serving.

Nutrition: calories: 509 carbohydrates: 5g fat: 45g protein: 23g

DINNER CHAFFLE RECIPES

Italian Sausage Chaffles

Preparation time: 10 minutes

Cooking Time: 8 Minutes

Servings: 2

Ingredients:

- 1 egg, beaten
- 1 cup cheddar cheese, shredded
- ¼ cup Parmesan cheese, grated
- 1 lb. Italian sausage, crumbled
- 2 teaspoons baking powder
- 1 cup almond flour

Directions:

1. Preheat your waffle maker.
2. Mix all the ingredients in a bowl.
3. Pour half of the mixture into the waffle maker.
4. Cover and cooking for minutes.
5. Transfer to a plate.
6. Let cool to make it crispy.
7. Do the same steps to make the next chaffle.

Nutrition: Carbohydrates: 1 g Fats: 62 g Proteins: 28 g Calories: 680

Chaffles With Strawberry Frosty

Preparation time: 10 minutes

Cooking Time: 5 Minutes

Servings:2

Ingredients:

- 1 cup frozen strawberries
- 1/2 cup Heavy cream
- 1 tsp. stevia
- 1 scoop protein powder
- 3 keto chaffles

Directions:

1. Mix together all ingredients in a mixing bowl.
2. Pour mixture in silicone molds and freeze in a freezer for about 4 hours to set.
3. Once frosty is set, top on keto chaffles and enjoy!

Nutrition: Carbohydrates: 9 g Fats: 36 g Proteins: 32 g Calories: 474

Pecan Pumpkin Chaffle

Preparation time: 20 minutes

Cooking Time: 15 Minutes

Servings: 2

Ingredients:

- 1 egg
- 2 tbsp. pecans, toasted and chopped
- 2 tbsp. almond flour
- 1 tsp. erythritol
- 1/4 tsp. pumpkin pie spice
- 1 tbsp. pumpkin puree
- 1/2 cup Mozzarella cheese, grated

Directions:

1. Preheat your waffle maker.
2. Beat egg in a small bowl.
3. Add remaining ingredients and mix well.
4. Spray waffle maker with cooking spray.
5. Pour half batter in the hot waffle maker and cooking for minutes or until golden brown. Repeat with the remaining batter.
6. Serve and enjoy.

Nutrition: Calories: 240 Total Fat: 16 g Protein: 21 g Total Carbs: 3g

Fiber: 1g Net Carbs: 2g

Savory Gruyere & Chives Chaffles

Preparation time: 20 minutes

Cooking Time: 14 Minutes

Servings: 2

Ingredients:

- 2 eggs, beaten
- 1 cup finely grated Gruyere cheese
- 2 tbsp. finely grated cheddar cheese
- 1/8 tsp. freshly ground black pepper
- 3 tbsp. minced fresh chives + more for garnishing
- 2 sunshine fried eggs for topping

Directions:

1. Preheat the waffle iron.
2. In a medium bowl, mix the eggs, cheeses, black pepper, and chives.
3. Open the iron and pour in half of the mixture.
4. Close the iron and cooking until brown and crispy, 7 minutes.
5. Remove the chaffle onto a plate and set aside.
6. Make another chaffle using the remaining mixture.
7. Top each chaffle with one fried egg each, garnish with the chives and serve.

Nutrition: Calories: 402 Total Fat: 30g Protein: 30g Total Carbs: 3g Fiber: 1g Net Carbs: 2g

Swiss Bacon Chaffle

Preparation time: 10 minutes

Cooking Time: 8 Minutes

Servings: 2

Ingredients:

- 1 egg
- ½ cup Swiss cheese
- 2 tablespoons cooked crumbled bacon

Directions:

1. Preheat your waffle maker.
2. Beat the egg in a bowl.
3. Stir in the cheese and bacon.
4. Pour half of the mixture into the device.
5. Close and cooking for 4 minutes.
6. Cooking the second chaffle using the same steps.

Nutrition: Calories: 317 Total Fat: 18g Protein: 38g

Total Carbs: 0g

Fiber: 0g Net Carbs: 0g

Bacon, Olives & Cheddar Chaffle

Preparation time: 10 minutes

Cooking Time: 8 Minutes

Servings: 2

Ingredients:

- 1 egg
- ½ cup cheddar cheese, shredded
- 1 tablespoon black olives, chopped
- 1 tablespoon bacon bits

Directions:

1. Plug in your waffle maker.
2. In a bowl, beat the egg and stir in the cheese.
3. Add the black olives and bacon bits.
4. Mix well.
5. Add half of the mixture into the waffle maker.
6. Cover and cooking for 4 minutes.
7. Open and transfer to a plate.
8. Let cool for 2 minutes.
9. Cooking the other chaffle using the remaining batter.

Nutrition: Calories: 733 Total Fat: 53g Protein: 54g
Total Carbs: 10g
Fiber: 6g Net Carbs: 4g

Garlic Chaffle

Servings: 2

Cooking Time: 8 Minutes

Ingredients:

- 1 egg
- ½ cup cheddar cheese, beaten
- 1 teaspoon coconut flour
- Pinch garlic powder

Directions:

1. Plug in your waffle maker.
2. Beat the egg in a bowl.
3. Stir in the rest of the ingredients.
4. Pour half of the batter into your waffle maker.
5. Cooking for 4 minutes.
6. Remove the waffle and let sit for 2 minutes.
7. Do the same steps with the remaining batter.

Nutrition: Calories 273, Carbs 5.7 g, Fat 12 g, Protein 34 g, Sodium 689 mg, Sugar 0 g

Herby Chaffle Snacks

Preparation time: 30 minutes

Cooking Time: 28 Minutes

Servings: 4

Ingredients:

- 1 egg, beaten
- ½ cup finely grated Monterey Jack cheese
- ¼ cup finely grated Parmesan cheese
- ½ tsp. dried mixed herbs

Directions:

1. Preheat the waffle iron.
2. Mix all the ingredients in a medium bowl
3. Open the iron and pour in a quarter of the mixture. Close and cooking until crispy, 7 minutes.
4. Remove the chaffle onto a plate and make 3 more with the rest of the ingredients.
5. Cut each chaffle into wedges and plate.
6. Allow cooling and serve.

Nutrition: Calories 203, Carbs 4.7 g, Fat 10 g, Protein 25 g, Sodium 479 mg, Sugar 0 g

Zucchini Chaffle

Preparation time: 10 minutes

Cooking Time: 8 Minutes

Servings: 2

Ingredients:

- 1 cup zucchini, grated
- ¼ cup Mozzarella cheese, shredded
- 1 egg, beaten
- ½ cup Parmesan cheese, shredded
- 1 teaspoon dried basil
- Salt and pepper to taste

Directions:

1. Preheat your waffle maker.
2. Sprinkle pinch of salt over the zucchini and mix.
3. Let sit for 2 minutes.
4. Wrap zucchini with paper towel and squeeze to get rid of water.
5. Transfer to a bowl and stir in the rest of the ingredients.
6. Pour half of the mixture into the waffle maker.
7. Close the device.
8. Cooking for 4 minutes.
9. Make the second chaffle following the same steps.

Nutrition: Calories 273, Carbs 6 g, Fat 11 g, Protein 37 g, Sodium 714 mg, Sugar 0 g

Pumpkin Chaffle With Frosting

Preparation time: 20 minutes

Cooking Time: 15 Minutes

Servings: 2

Ingredients:

- 1 egg, lightly beaten
- 1 tbsp. sugar-free pumpkin puree
- 1/4 tsp. pumpkin pie spice
- 1/2 cup Mozzarella cheese, shredded

For frosting:

- 1/2 tsp. vanilla
- 2 tbsp. Swerve
- 2 tbsp. cream cheese, softened

Directions:

1. Preheat your waffle maker.
2. Add egg in a bowl and whisk well.
3. Add pumpkin puree, pumpkin pie spice, and cheese and stir well.
4. Spray waffle maker with cooking spray.
5. Pour 1/2 of the batter in the hot waffle maker and cooking for 3-4 minutes or until golden brown. Repeat with the remaining batter.
6. In a small bowl, mix all frosting ingredients until smooth.

7. Add frosting on top of hot chaffles and serve.

Nutrition: Calories 366, Carbs 6 g, Fat 19 g, Protein 43 g, Sodium 1183 mg, Sugar 0 g